Photographs
Colin Jeal
David Alderton

Front cover painting by:
Julie Stooks

We would like to thank the following for permission to photograph their stock:
Hansards Pet Centre, Romsey

Your First
PARROT

CONTENTS

©1996
by Kingdom
Books
PO7 6AR
ENGLAND

your first parrot

Kingdom Books is an imprint of T.F.H. Publications   Printed in England.

HISTORY

Parrots and parrot-type birds have been popular pets through the ages. The Asiatic parakeets were brought into Europe during the time of Alexander the Great and one, the Alexandrine parakeet, derives its name from him.

As explorers and traders opened up the world, sailors and travellers to Africa, Asia and the Americas brought back various members of the parrot family. Later the Australian cockatoos, parakeets and lorikeets were brought back and quickly achieved popularity. Their colourful plumage, longevity and ability to mimic the sounds around them ensured a ready market at home.

The umbrella cockatoo is not such a good talker as the better-known sulphur-crested, but its voice is generally less strident.

The United States was the natural habitat of only one parrot-type bird: the Carolina parakeet. This bird was hunted for its decorative plumage to such an exent that it is now extinct.

Historically, caged birds were kept by the aristocracy. Most ordinary people did not discover the charms of caged birds until the early nineteenth century.

Parrot-type birds are commonly reputed to live to a grand old age. Although many of them do live to be 50 years old or more, stories of parrots living to be 75 or 100 should be taken with a pinch of salt. Occasionally a bird may reach such a great age, but only very rarely. Considering the potential long life of a parrot, the high purchase price is justifiable; the care and feeding of the bird are not particularly expensive. Potential keepers should keep the parrot's likely life span in mind before they buy one as a pet. Unlike a hamster, which may die within a year or two, a properly-kept parrot is a long-term commitment of time, energy and finance.

A pair of grey-cheeked parakeets standing comfortably on their natural perch.

WHY A PARROT?

I know of no more satisfying or rewarding pet than a tame and intelligent bird of the parrot family. With its ability to mimic the human voice and its comical ways, it furnishes an endless source of amusement for its owner and friends. It can also bring about some awfully embarrassing situations.

I remember one occasion in a pet shop several years ago when a junior school teacher brought her class of 30 children to see the birds and animals that were on sale there. The children were everywhere and into everything and pandemonium ruled! When the confusion was at its height a huge scarlet macaw added its voice to the general bedlam. To calm it, the owner of the shop took the bird out of its cage and put it on her wrist. A few minutes later, the teacher lined the children up to leave. As the last child marched out of the door the teacher said, 'Thank you so much, I hope we haven't been too much trouble.' The shop owner replied, 'Not at all.' At the same time the macaw shrieked in unmistakable syllables, 'Oh, yeah! Haw-haw-haw-haw.'

They say that parrots cannot think but only mimic familiar sounds. I sometimes wonder...

Some parrots are quite friendly with everybody and some are one-person birds. Most have distinct likes and dislikes, being quite fond of some people and antagonistic to others. Some like men and dislike women, others the reverse. As a general rule, a female bird will become more attached to men and a male bird more attached to women. They are all rather temperamental and unpredictable and there is no accounting for some of their actions. As a rule, if they have good care and the proper diet, they become quite docile and their amusing ways soon make them a real part of the family.

The joy you derive from your parrot will be in proportion to the amount of care and training you give it. After all, you cannot expect your parrot to be a docile and affectionate pet if it is unhealthy or frightened of you.

'Why fly when you can ride?' A scarlet macaw enjoys its owner's company.

WHICH PARROT?

What is a parrot? Walking into your local pet shop and enthusiastically telling the proprietor you want to purchase a parrot can be a little risky. From the majestic green-winged macaw to the exquisite purple-crowned lorikeet, parrot-like birds vary tremendously in size, type, required care, availability and cost. The macaw, for instance, is 90cm long, while the tiny lorikeet is only 15cm.

Parrots belong to the order **Psittaciformes**. Regardless of size, colour or continent of origin, all members of this order have hooked bills, mallet-shaped tongues, harsh voices, powerful legs and the ability to mimic. The order is then subdivided many times into smaller and more specific groups, the most important of which are species and subspecies. All members of a species look similar and produce progeny which look alike. The difference between one subspecies and the next may be based on geography, size, and/or colour patterns.

For the bird lover who hopes to find the ideal parrot, perhaps visiting a bird show or a local bird sanctuary would prove helpful. Seeing how these remarkable animals live can give a potential owner insights that the written word or photograph cannot.

POPULAR PARROTS

No pet shop or aviary could possibly offer every kind of parrot; many parrots are now endangered species, rare even within their original habitats. Others have been bred successfully in captivity, so are easier to acquire.

Purchase prices vary considerably, depending on what kind of parrot you want. Learn as much as you can about the species you like before buying it.

A Quaker, or Monk, parakeet of the blue variety.

It is not possible to list every species and subspecies of parrot in the world in a book this size, but I have dealt with some of the parrots that are popular within the pet world. A potential owner may find even some of these birds difficult to locate but, by getting to know breeders and dealers, and having a lot of patience, you will achieve success.

For the sake of our discussion, the parrot family can be divided into two generic groups: parakeets and parrots. The main difference between the two groups is that the parrot has a shorter tail. The budgerigar (called the parakeet in the United States) is aptly described as a parakeet because of its long tail. The budgie, as it is called affectionately the bird world over, is the most popular of all the parrot-family birds.

Parakeets

Let us discuss parakeets other than the little budgie and make continental distinctions between them. There are three continents to consider: Asia, Australia and South America.

Asian Parakeets: These parakeets originate in the Indian subcontinent and nearby countries. The group consists of approximately 35 species and subspecies, and all are noted for their long tails and ringed necks. Asian parakeets vary in availability.

The largest Asian parakeet is the Alexandrine parakeet, which measures approximately 53cm and therefore requires a considerable amount of flying space. Alexandrines tend to breed more consistently than many of their ringnecked cousins.

The Indian ringneck or Bengal parakeet is another promising member of this group. These birds can be kept singly and are a popular option for parakeet keepers. Nearly 40cm in length, they are the most widely-bred of all parakeets and prove hardy and easy to acclimatise.

Other Asian parakeets are the moustached parakeet and plum-headed parakeet. While just as attractive as the Indian and Alexandrine parakeets, these birds are not so easy to breed and therefore are less commonly kept.

Australian Parakeets: These richly-coloured Aussies are a vigorous lot, breeding prolifically when cared for correctly. The group can be subdivided into three categories: grass parakeets, rosellas or broadtails, and 'others'.

Grass parakeets are conveniently-sized, beautifully-plumaged birds that have proved to be good breeders in captivity. They are therefore

Above: At 23cm long, the Senegal parrot is one of the smaller African parrots.

Opposite: A magnificent scarlet macaw.

deservedly popular in the bird world, epitomising the ideal aviary bird. The various species require very similar care. Examples include the blue-winged grass parakeet, the elegant grass parakeet, Bourke's parakeet, the splendid grass parakeet, and the turquoisine grass parakeet. These birds range from 20-23cm in length and the predominant colour is green or olive green. Different species have identifying coloured markings, such as chestnut shoulders, scarlet chests or blue wings.

Rosellas, the second group of Australian parakeets, exhibit a characteristic broad tail; indeed, they are sometimes referred to as 'broadtails'. Averaging 32cm in length, rosellas are good-looking and relatively easy to buy from pet shops. They are not recommended for those inexperienced in breeding birds.
Among the most popular rosellas are the common rosella, crimson rosella, golden-mantled rosella, mealy rosella and western rosella. Spangled mantles grace the rosellas and, along with the broad tails, are hallmarks of the species.

The second category of Australian parakeets includes the cockatiel, king parakeet, Princess Alexandra parakeet, red-rumped parakeet and rock pebbler parakeet.

The increasingly popular cockatiel is a very good choice for you as a new parakeet keeper, whether or not you plan to breed your birds. The cockatiel is an ideal single pet and is most adaptable. Many owners have had excellent success with teaching this bird a few words and phrases. The colour possibilities and overall appearance of the species are stunning, and this and its other qualities make it a very popular choice.

The red-rumped parakeet is also popular with parrot keepers, who delight in its colourful plumage, ease of breeding and general hardiness. These parakeets are notably gregarious and will tolerate many different species in their aviary, including finches, cockatiels and other parakeets.

South American Parakeets: Not all the parakeets in this flock originate in South America; some come from Central America and Mexico. This group can be subdivided into two: conures and conurine parakeets.

Conures have a distinctive look about them. The conure's head and beak are exceptionally large, while the body is thin and the tail tapers. Conures vary greatly in size, ranging from 23-53cm in length. Although the conure does not generally breed profusely in captivity, it is an easy bird to care for and feed, proving a hardy, adaptable pet. Overall green predominates, but splashes of white, orange, red, yellow and/or blue liven up the plumages. Some of the conures are more popular than others.

Conures can be found throughout a large part of Central and South America. From Panama we meet the brown-eared conure; from Brazil, the golden-crowned conure; from Argentina, the Pantagonian conure; from South America, Quaker's conure. Other popular conures include Petz's conure, the nanday conure, the jenday conure, Queen of Bavaria conure, the white-eared conure and the red-bellied conure.

Conurine parakeets are fairly small and generally are considered close relatives to conures. Sweet and peace-loving in nature, the 16 or more species bunched under this parakeet umbrella are popular pets, despite their somewhat dull colouration. Most owners have good experience with keeping conurine parakeets singly, although pairs are favoured by fanciers, due to their moderate size. Among the conurine parakeets are the bee bee parakeet, canary-winged parakeet and white-winged parakeet. These are the most accessible of the domesticated conurine parakeets.

Parrots

Daring and adventurous parrot enthusiasts seeking a larger, more dramatic-appearing bird must look to the second group, which we refer to as 'parrots and parrot-like species'. (This is not to suggest that the aforementioned parakeets are not parrots; they certainly are.) Anyone hearing the term 'parrot' probably thinks of the first two genus in this group: the African grey parrot and the Amazon parrot.

African Grey Parrot: Sometimes called the grey parrot, this parrot makes the best pet of all the large parrots. Notably affectionate and intelligent, the African grey is a good mimic, with astonishing ability. Taming and training is

The African grey parrot makes the best pet of all the large parrots.

best undertaken when the bird is still young, as adults can be more wilful and difficult to train. In length, the grey parrot is 33cm. The adult plumage is pale grey, marked with lighter and darker shades of grey and black on the body. The tail feathers range from bright red to dull maroon. The principal diet consists of seeds, nuts and fruits. Demand for the grey parrot as a pet continues to grow, as this bird has proved to be a better talker and more intelligent than the Amazon parrot.

Amazon Parrots: Amazons were once widely-distributed across the South American continent, the only continent on which they occur naturally. All Amazons belong to the genus *Amazona*, which is divided into about 27 species. Some of the great Amazons are extinct today and many, such as the St Lucia or Puerto Rico Amazon, exist only on one island. Medium in size, Amazons range from 25-36cm and are principally green in colour. Their tails are slightly rounded and their wings are round and broad. As well as being superior talkers they are proficient, even acrobatic, climbers. However, they are subject to whims and fleeting moments of bad temper and have powerful screeches which they use regularly with gusto.

Among the more popular of the Amazons are the blue-fronted, orange-wing, mealy, red-fronted, double yellow-headed, and yellow-fronted. The blue-fronted and orange-wing are the most commonly kept Amazons.

Others: There are other parrots, neither greys nor Amazons, that should be counted here. The grand eclectus parrot, Maximillian's parrot, the yellow-bellied Senegal parrot and the vernal hanging parrot are all notable and pleasant parrots that are kept in captivity. The least commonly kept of these is the grand eclectus, an expensive and, unfortunately, scarce bird. This bird, too, is highly attractive, colourful and quite amenable to captivity.

Cockatoos: Native to Australia and the islands of the South Pacific, the cockatoo is unique for its expressive head crest. The colour is mostly white, sometimes with greyish shades throughout. A few cockatoos are black or grey. Their size varies from 30-76cm. Cockatoos are supreme entertainers, clown- or dancer-like in their amusing, often musical, antics. They are long-lived, intelligent birds, strong in body and voice. Ideally, cockatoos are kept in aviaries since they are very active and need room for exercise.

Of the cockatoo species, the umbrella cockatoo is among the most plentiful. It was found originally on the islands located northwest of New Guinea. The umbrella cockatoo is large and white, with yellow suffusion under the wings and tail. Cockatoos can be fussy eaters, and the umbrella is one of the worst for this. Sunflower seeds, apples and corn on the cob are among its favourite foods.

Considered the aristocrat of the genus, the greater sulphur-crested cockatoo can be as long as 56cm and is truly splendid in its plumage. This bird is unmistakable in its dignity and stunning appearance.

Goffin's cockatoo is among the smallest of the genus, measuring only 30cm in length. Its popularity in the pet world is attributed to its convenient size, its appealing looks and its pleasant disposition.

Another fairly small cockatoo is the roseate cockatoo or galah. This is a clean, pleasant pet that delights its owners with its charming demonstrations of intelligence and playfulness.

Lories: The subfamily known as **Loriinae** contains lories, lorikeets and the closely-related lorilets and fig parrots. These are attractive, brilliantly-coloured parrots whose characteristic diet is fruit and nectar; they are not seed-eaters like most other parrots. Birds in this group have peculiar brush-like tongues that enable them to lap up nectar in a cat-like way. They survive on a chiefly liquid diet: nectar syrup, honey and evaporated milk. Fresh food must be provided daily without exception.

Since the lory has difficulty keeping itself tidy in a confined space, it should be given as much room as possible.

Lories and lorikeets are delightful birds, highly comical and amusing to watch. While these parrots enjoy each other's company, they tend to be 'gang-oriented' and may assault another bird kept in the same cage.

At one time, when its feeding habits were less understood, the lory was considered a specialist's bird. Today, while it is true that lories require more experience and daily attention than other parrots, they are as long-lived, intelligent and enjoyable as their cousins. The novice bird keeper must be aware of the lory's powerful bite: correct handling is particularly important. While any lory kept correctly can be a delight to its owner, the birds are generally deemed unpredictable and excitable. I would not recommend that you buy a lory until you have more experience of parrots.

Macaws: The macaw is the largest member of the parrot family, ranging in size from 36-91cm. The largest is the exquisite hyacinth macaw, a dazzling blue bird, comparable in appearance and intelligence to any of the 24 species of the macaw genus *Ara*.

The macaw's plumage is undeniably brilliant, ranging in colour from the deep, lush blue of the hyacinth macaw to the sparkling red of the scarlet macaw. The characteristics of the genus include large, pointed beaks, pointed and lengthy tails, full plumage and bald cheek patches on the face. However, they are not everyone's choice, and are not recommended for novices. They are very expensive and can be nasty and wilful, not to mention destructive. In all fairness, they can also be wonderful companions, with the charm and affection of the best kitten or puppy. They bond with their owners and require much attention. An ignored macaw will

Macaws, like this beautiful blue and yellow, are magnificent in colour, but they can be temperamental and are not recommended for beginners.

make its discontent known; its screech is as bad as its bite.

The hyacinth macaw is a rare bird that is much in demand. Some members of the genus are easier to obtain, such as the blue and yellow macaw, the scarlet macaw, and the red and blue macaw.

Lovebirds: Most lovebirds come from Africa, where they live in the dry savanna regions. They are among the smaller parrots and have short tails. Their subtly-shaded, brightly-coloured plumage, gregarious natures and undemanding habits have earned them a prominent place with bird keepers. Once they are acclimatised, care is simple compared to that of most other parrots.

Lovebirds are usually housed in cages, since they fit comfortably into standard-sized cages. The average lovebird is 12-15cm long. They also do well in aviaries and reproduce quite easily in captivity.

Bird fanciers find the lovebird fascinating to observe. One of the things that makes it so interesting is the way it constructs its nest in the nest box that you provide, transporting twigs and straw under its wings. The largest lovebird, the Abyssinian or black-winged lovebird, makes a good cage and aviary bird but proves less easy to breed. The Aby is easy to train and gets on well with other birds and is a favourite with bird keepers.

The African grey parrot is notably affectionate and intelligent, and the best mimic of all.

Alexandrine parakeets, *Psittacula eupatria*, in an outdoor aviary.

The black-masked lovebird has been kept widely for many years in the United States. Its interesting plumage colouration and breeding behaviour have won it popularity and high acclaim.

One of the most accessible of lovebirds is the peach-faced lovebird. As with most lovebirds, breeding pairs prove quarrelsome and are best housed separately from other birds to prevent fighting. One or two of the species are among the noisiest representatives of the parrot family.

Fischer's lovebirds, like black-masked lovebirds, are popular and hardy. They prefer warm ambient temperatures, and require a very dry environment. Being easy-to-care-for, prolific birds, they are highly recommended to the novice parrot keeper.

At only 13cm long, the Mexican parrotlet is one of the smallest species of parrot.

HOUSING

There are several things to remember as far as the housing of parrot-type birds is concerned. Generally speaking, the more room a parrot-type bird (or any other bird for that matter) can be given, the better. I much prefer putting a bird on a stand to confining it in a cage. A stand gives the bird more freedom of movement and allows it more exercise, resulting in a healthier, happier bird.

Larger birds can be trained to stay on a stand. The stand should have a wooden perch and the ends of it should be capped with metal so that your parrot cannot chew it to pieces. Pet shops sell the best stands, which are available in a variety of sizes and styles.

However, for some birds, especially for young, untamed parrots, a cage is more practical and may even be necessary. When a cage is used, care should be taken to have one that is large enough so that the bird has enough room to exercise. A cage that is big enough for one of the smaller Amazon parrots would not be adequate for one of the larger macaws or cockatoos. The cage is too small if the bird cannot stand in the centre of the middle perch and flap its wings without touching the bars of the cage. In other words, the cage should be considerably wider than the wing span of the bird. Parrot-type birds exercise by standing on the perch and flapping their wings vigorously. They should be given every opportunity to do this.

Many cages come fitted with a swing. If it interferes with the bird's exercise, you should take it out. Try to ensure that each perch is of a different diameter, as this gives your parrot's feet a rest and change. Square perches with the corners smoothly rounded off are easier for the parrot's feet to grip and less tiring than completely round ones.

A metal cage will need a coat of paint occasionally to prevent corrosion. Care should be taken to use enamel or some kind of paint that does not contain lead or other toxic ingredients. Parrots are notorious for chewing everything within reach. Inevitably, they will chew on their cages, sometimes getting bits of paint in their mouths. Parrots are extremely sensitive to lead so, if the paint on the cage contains lead, you may have a very sick, or even dead, bird on your hands. If you have a stainless steel cage you do not need to worry about painting.

Some people say that a parrot's cage should be enclosed on three sides and have wire on one side only, so that the bird can look in only one direction, without any distractions. This is ideal while you are training the bird and teaching it to talk. However, as a general rule, it would be very confining for a bird to be able to look in only one direction, and certainly not conducive to the maximum comfort and happiness of your pet. The most reliable source for the bird's cage is your local pet shop. Pet shops offer a wide range of cages and indoor aviaries. You may even choose to have a cage made for your bird.

CLEANING

One other very important thing to remember is to clean the parrot's cage or quarters. In the wild, the parrot can move about from place to place, so clean quarters are no problem; in captivity, it is completely dependent on its keeper for clean quarters. Dirty quarters may be a breeding place for parasites and disease.

Clean out the cage at least every other day. It should have a removable tray, covered with a piece of paper cut to size, which in turn should be covered with a generous amount of clean bird sand. The sand absorbs the moisture in the droppings, making conditions more sanitary and cleaning easier. Grit to aid the bird's digestion should not be placed on the floor as the bird may ingest parasites while picking it up.

Food and water dishes should be cleaned out regularly. It is particularly important to provide fresh water daily, otherwise there is danger of contamination and disease. In addition to this routine cleaning, the cage should be dismantled and disinfected from time to time. This is a precaution against disease and against mites that may get on your bird (perhaps brought in on bird seed) and may breed in the crevices of the cage. A good method of disinfecting the cage is to scald the various parts of it with boiling water and a generous amount of a good household disinfectant. When the cage is thoroughly dry, dust a mite-killing powder, obtainable from your local pet dealer, into the crevices of the cage and under the removable tray.

Covering your bird at night will help to protect it from draughts and provide a 'night and day'. The cover should not prevent fresh air getting to your parrot. Covers can also help to settle a nervous bird at night.

OUTDOOR KEEPING

Parrot owners living in the country may want to construct outdoor pens for their pets to use in warm weather. This is an excellent way to make sure your bird gets enough exercise, fresh air and sunlight. A shelter should be provided so that the bird can get out of the direct sunlight and rain if it so desires. Many birds enjoy a light shower of warm rain, however.

Some parrot-type birds can be given their freedom safely, but this is risky unless you are sure of your bird's tameness. My father had a macaw that had the freedom of the farm for several years and was quite tame and happy to stay near without being confined. I have also known of double yellow-headed Amazon parrots that were given their freedom and stayed close by. It is a risk to try this unless your bird is quite tame.

Whatever provision you make for your bird, it is important that you do not confine it where it cannot get out of a direct draught or out of direct sunlight. Parrot-family birds are subject to colds and are likely to catch cold if left in a draught. They may also suffer from sunstroke if they cannot get out of the direct sunlight. Either of these may prove to be fatal. Many species of parrot will live outside all year round and breed if provided with a sturdy shelter. Some species require additional heating during the winter months.

If you intend to keep parrots outside, please consider the distance from your neighbour's house. Not everyone appreciates the screech of a parrot, and you may find yourself fighting a legal battle if they are too noisy.

An outdoor aviary suitable for smaller species, such as lovebirds or grass parakeets. Always make sure that your birds can keep out of draughts and direct sunlight.

The head patterns and colouration of Amazon parrots can vary greatly, although their basic colour is predominantly green.

FEEDING

In discussing the feeding of parrot-family birds, I believe that what you don't do is more important than what you do. It is important to remember that in the wild state most parrot-family birds are seed-eaters and vegetarians. (There are exceptions to seed-eating parrots, the lories being a notable example.) The birds' digestive systems are not equipped to take care of greasy, fatty foods. Instead of trying to list all of the things that should not be fed to parrots let me simply say that parrots should be given only the diet set out below. Above all, do not feed left-over table scraps and rich, greasy foods.

The diet of most of the larger parrot-family birds should consist of equal parts of seeds, green foods and fruits. The seed part of their diet should be made up of a mixture of sunflower seed, oats, canary seed and millet. This is the staple seed diet. To this you can add other seeds such as corn, wheat, buckwheat, hemp, peanuts and other varieties of nuts. The birds can easily crack the hard shells with their powerful bills. Vitamins may be added to the seed mixtures in cold weather. About a teaspoonful should be added to a pint of seed and mixed thoroughly before it is given to the bird.

Parrots should have some green foods regularly. Most fresh green garden vegetables are excellent. Many parrots are particularly fond of corn on the cob when it is in the milk stage. The greens should be fed uncooked and unseasoned, but should be washed thoroughly so that any poisonous sprays may be washed off. About a third of a parrot's diet should consist of non-citrus fruit such as cherries, berries, grapes and apples. Citrus fruit should be fed sparingly, if at all. As an occasional treat, give a piece of wholewheat bread or a cracker.

A piece of cuttlebone should be available to the parrot at all times. This provides the calcium necessary for the building of bone, beak and feathers. Additionally, provide a supply of grit. This is an absolute necessity. Parrots, like other birds, store grit in their gizzards and use it to grind their food. They can get along without a fresh supply for a short period of time but, if deprived of it for any extended period, will sicken and die.

Many good diet supplements for parrot-type birds are available. It is not absolutely necessary to provide a supplement but it may help to maintain the health and vigour of your bird, particularly in the winter months.

The ease with which you train your bird to talk or to do tricks depends on how tame it is. Training and taming will depend on the intelligence, disposition and capabilities of the individual bird and the patience of the trainer. Age is another important factor; a young parrot is much easier to train than an old one. The sex of a bird apparently has no bearing on the matter: females learn just as readily as males.

The first step in training a parrot is taming it, for you cannot train a wild bird. The younger the bird and the more attention it has had from people, the easier this task will be. If you get a bird that has been hand-reared you will have no problem taming but, if you get an older bird that has recently been caught or has been neglected, you will need a considerable amount of patience to tame it. However, it is much more likely that you will get a young bird that has not had much experience with people, and is rather scared and completely bewildered by its recent changes in environment.

TAMING

To tame your bird you must first win its confidence. The bird must know that you do not intend to harm it when you enter the room or approach the cage. A new bird should be allowed to rest and become accustomed to its surroundings for a day or two before any effort is made to tame it.

One of the first steps in taming a bird is to put it in a place where it will have the frequent company of people. In this way, it will become used to human companionship.

After the first day or so, make a point to be near the cage as much as possible and talk to the bird in quiet and reassuring tones. Do not make any quick movements near the bird; move slowly and deliberately. Place your hands on the cage from time to time, all the while talking to the bird. After a few days, when the bird has become accustomed to this, open the cage door slowly and put your hand inside. Repeat this several times a day for a week or so. Soon your parrot will become accustomed to your hand and will lose its fear of you.

The power of hunger and the use of food in obtaining confidence and overcoming fear is frequently overlooked in the taming of any bird or animal. I do **not** mean that you should starve your bird unnecessarily. However, when your bird learns that you are the one to whom it must look for food, it will come to have confidence in you more quickly. If a hungry bird has the choice of eating out of your hand or not at all, it is likely to eat out of your hand. Do not overdo this to the point where you endanger your

Most parrots are clever at mimicking the sounds around them, but if you want to teach your pet to talk, you must have lots of patience.

bird's health or make it paranoid and uncomfortable. In an extremely wild bird, fear can be more powerful than hunger.

It can be helpful to take all food out of the cage or away from the bird when it has had its evening feed. Parrots tend to eat first thing in the morning so, with the food unavailable to them until you replace it, they will get pretty hungry. Do not wait too long to replace the food but, when you do so, let your hands linger around the feed dish for a few moments. Repeat this procedure for several days and then, one day when you have a little extra time, put the feed dish within your parrot's reach and keep it in your hand. Eventually, depending on how hungry and how confident it is, your parrot will eat out of the dish that you are holding. Do not make a sudden movement or a loud noise or you will undo all that you have accomplished.

Birds kept alone can be tamed more easily than those kept with other birds. If you are trying to tame more than one bird, you will have more success if you keep them in separate cages. It will be better if they are not even in the same room. If other birds are present, the bird you are trying to tame will not become dependent on human companionship but will rely on that of the other birds. When your birds are thoroughly tamed and trained it will not do any harm to keep them together.

TALKING

One of the questions every new parrot owner asks is, 'How do I teach my bird to talk?' The answer is simple, but requires patience: by repeating to it again and again what you want it to say. You can start doing this while you are still taming your bird. In teaching a bird to talk, repeat the word or phrase (it is better to start with a single word, maybe the parrot's name) over and over as often as you can. Say it first thing in the morning and after the lights are out at night. Soon your bird will reward your patience by repeating it after you. When your bird has mastered its first word, start on a new word. The more a bird learns, the more quickly it learns.

At one time, it was believed that a parrot talked better if its tongue was split. If anything, this detracted from its talking (not to mention feeding) ability. It certainly did not improve upon the ability of parrot-family birds to mimic the sounds they hear. However, some people still come out with this, and you should refuse to listen to this advice.

During the past few years a number of cassette and compact-disc recordings have appeared on the market to help teach parrots to talk. These recordings can be used very effectively in training parrots and should be played over and over within the bird's hearing. One advantage is that they can be played repeatedly while you are away or are busy doing something else. However, a parrot becomes a member of the family and, I think, should be taught to say the names of family members and phrases that have some family significance. This is not possible when you teach your parrot to talk by means of a record.

LEARNING TRICKS

The best way to teach a parrot tricks is by rewarding a good performance with praise and a favourite food. Parrots can be taught many of the same tricks that dogs or other animals learn, such as to play dead or to shake hands. When they have been shown what is expected of them, they should be rewarded for a good performance.

A tame parrot will let you examine its tail feathers without too much fuss.

There are several things that you should know if the health, happiness and general well-being of your bird are to be maintained. First, remember that parrots are vegetarians. Their digestive systems are designed to take care of seeds, fruits and greens and not greasy or fatty foods. More pet parrots are killed by eating table scraps than from any other cause. A parrot may get by for a time on such unwholesome fare but eventually it will sicken and, unless put on a good diet, probably die.

Another very important thing to remember is that your bird should be kept in a comfortable place. The cage or stand should not be placed in a direct draught. As mentioned earlier, these birds catch colds very easily. A cold can soon go from bad to worse and may be fatal. Some tonics are available that may be given to your bird to combat a cold but, if your bird develops a bad cold in spite of your efforts, I would strongly advise that a veterinary surgeon be consulted. He can prescribe a remedy that will prove more effective than your home ones.

Be careful not to place your parrot so that it cannot get out of direct sunlight. Parrots are subject to sunstroke and may fall victim to the direct rays of the sun if they cannot get out of them. Sunstroke could be fatal.

Never underestimate the importance of cleanliness in the bird's living quarters.

BATHS

A question often asked by the new parrot owner is, 'Do parrots bathe?' This question cannot be answered with a simple 'yes' or 'no'. Some parrots bathe in a shallow dish of water; others do not. For the first few weeks that you have it give your parrot the opportunity to bathe. Provide a shallow dish that is not too light or slippery. An earthenware saucer intended for a large flower pot is ideal. These saucers are about the right depth, heavy enough not to tip up easily, and have a rough surface so that the parrot is unlikely to slip.

If, after a reasonable trial period, you find that your bird will not bathe you should spray it with a fine mist of water. This may be done by putting lukewarm water into an insect spray gun and spraying it directly on your bird; an atomiser or plastic spray bottle can also be used for this purpose. This should be done at least every other day.

The natural habitat of many parrots is the tropical rain forest. In these forests it rains practically every day, and the rain comes down through the

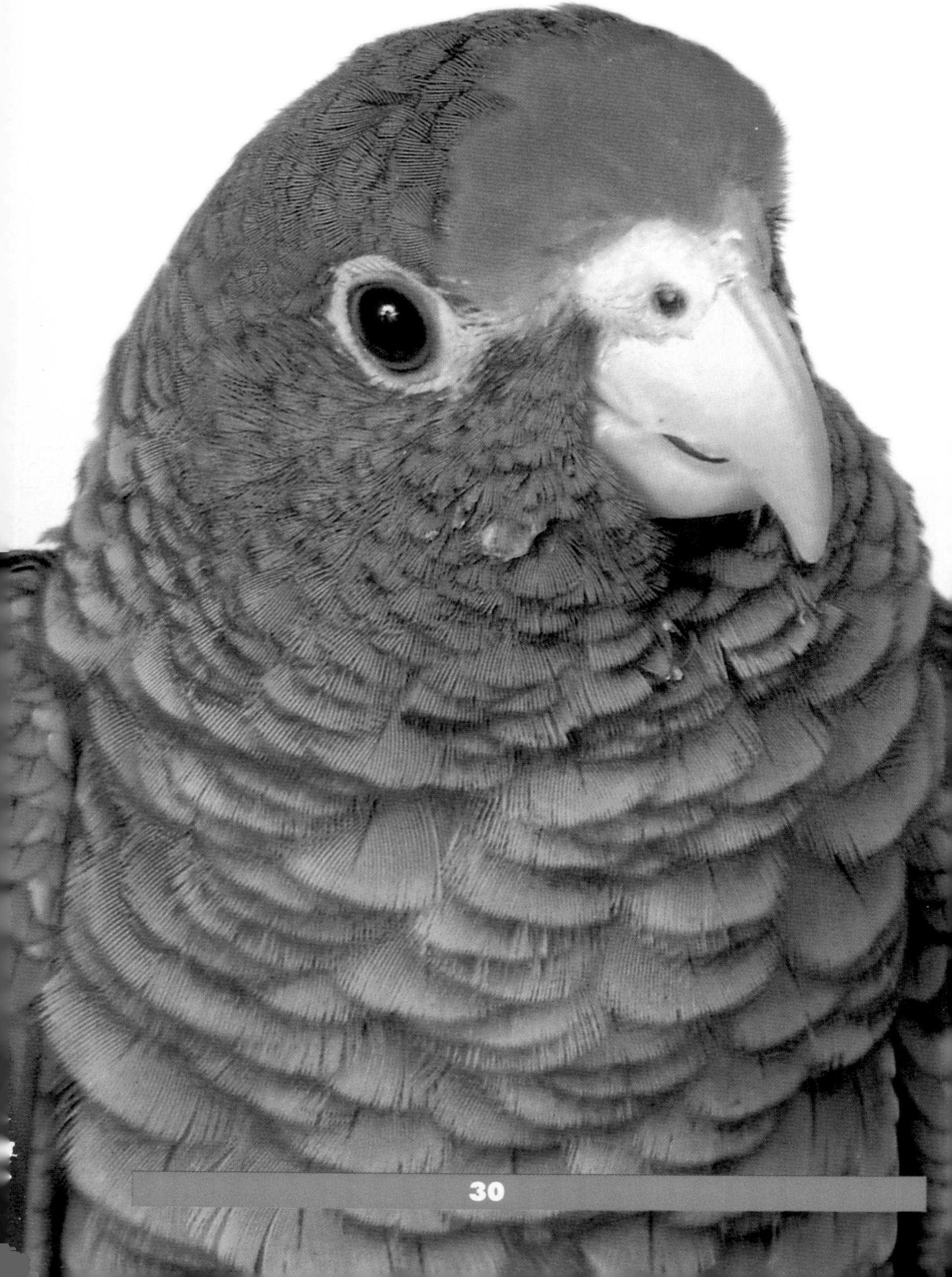

trees as a warm mist that thoroughly wets the birds' feathers. This is the only bath they take. You can duplicate this condition with your spray gun.

MITES

Remember that it is a wise precaution to obtain a good mite powder made especially for parrots and other cage birds. Many such powders are available on the market. About once a month both the parrot and its living quarters should be dusted liberally with this powder. The bird should have the powder blown up under its feathers and should be dusted all over. This is just a precaution. If any mites should happen to come in they will then be killed before they can become a problem.

If you should discover mites on your bird, just follow the directions on the mite powder packet. You should also disinfect the cage with boiling water as previously directed. If you keep your bird's quarters clean and dust both quarters and bird periodically you will not have to worry about mites. Any infestation will be nipped in the bud immediately.

Above: Birds that have been hand fed by humans grow up very tame.
Left: A Tucuman Amazon, *Amazona Tucumana*.

FIRST AID

Always remember: if your parrot becomes sick for any reason whatsoever the first thing to do is to keep it warm. The body temperature of birds is higher than that of many other animals so, when they are sick and run down, a thorough chilling can be disastrous. If possible, raise the ambient temperature to 30-32°C for a sick bird. You can do this by putting the bird into a box in which a large light bulb has been placed. The bulb will give off enough heat to keep the box warm. The bulb should be enclosed by wire and covered with a flame-resistant cloth so that the sick bird does not burn itself and is not made uncomfortable by the intense heat.

Pet supply companies offer hospital cages equipped with heating units, thermometers and thermostats. These cages are ideal for keeping a sick bird warm and are reasonably inexpensive.

GENERAL TIPS

People sometimes ask about clipping the bird's wing feathers so that it cannot fly. Many experts advise against this. If your bird is confined to a cage or a stand there is no need for it. If you set your bird at liberty, it would be extremely dangerous if it could not fly. Flight is its only means of escape from a dog, cat or other natural enemy.

The most essential thing for maintaining the happiness and general well-being of your parrot is that you give it the attention it requires. To be a good pet, any bird or animal requires a certain amount of attention. A parrot, deprived of other birds' companionship and human attention, soon grows dull, unresponsive and sullen. A neglected bird often turns to feather plucking, a disfiguring habit that is extremely hard to cure.

On the other hand if your bird receives adequate attention it will be a most rewarding and amusing pet. Spend a little while talking to it and playing with it every day if possible. Generally speaking, the more attention you give to any pet the more rewarding that pet is. This is certainly true of parrot-family birds.

In conclusion, let me advise the prospective parrot purchaser to be sure to get a good bird. With parrots, as with everything else, you get what you pay for. A young, partially-tamed bird will cost more than an old one but will be easier to tame and will be a more satisfying pet in the long run. Get your bird from a reputable pet shop and you will end up with a pet that will give you much enjoyment for very many years to come.

PARROTS OF THE WORLD
Joseph M Forshaw
ISBN 0-87666-995-3
PS-753

Every species and subspecies of parrot, including those now extinct, is described in this definitive work by an eminent ornithologist with a special interest in parrots. While designed to meet the needs of serious ornithologists and naturalists, it will be of interest to parrot fanciers throughout the world. The book is illustrated by William Cooper, whose paintings of birds have been acclaimed throughout the world.
Hardcover: 234 x 310mm, 584 pages, illustrated with colour and black and white drawings.

PARROTS AS A NEW PET
William Wentworth
ISBN 0-86622-434-3
TU-027

This colourful book, aimed at the beginner, sets out to cover all topics of interest to the enthusiast who is just starting to keep parrots as pets.
Softcover: 176 x 215mm, 64 pages, illustrated throughout with colour photos.

TAMING AND TRAINING PARROTS
Dr Edward J Mulawka
ISBN 0-86622-098-4
H-1019

Dr Mulawka's proven methods of parrot taming and training are detailed in this volume in step-by-step instructions. Information on how to choose the right parrot and care for it correctly is also given.
Hardcover: 136 x 202mm, 349 pages, illustrated throughout with colour and black and white photos.

KEEPING AND BREEDING PARROTS
Carl Aschenborn
ISBN 0-86622-960-4
TS110

This comprehensive book deals with parrots around the world and in captivity. The first few chapters deal with all aspects of parrot husbandry, and these are followed by descriptions of individual species, arranged by families and subfamilies. Illustrated throughout with colour photographs, this book is of immense value to the experienced aviculturalist and novice parrot keeper alike.
Hardcover: 214 x 276mm, 160 pages, over 100 colour photos.

THE WORLD OF MACAWS
Dieter Hoppe
ISBN 0-86622-125-5
H-1079

Macaws are probably the most familiar of all parrots. This book details each species and subspecies, and nearly all are illustrated with colour photographs or drawings. Range maps are also included to show their distribution in the wild. Information on all aspects of their care is covered, with topics such as selection, accommodation, feeding and breeding.
Hardcover: 210mm x 274mm, 144 pages, illustrated with 96 colour photos and drawings and black and white range maps.

PARRAKEETS OF THE WORLD
Dr Matthew M Vriends
ISBN 0-86622-733-4
H-101

A guide to parakeets throughout the world with chapters describing how to care for them in captivity.
Hardcover: 134 x 214mm, 384 pages, illustrated with many colour and black and white photos.